A Visit to Denmark

Sirpa White

ISBN 979-8-88832-969-6 (paperback)
ISBN 979-8-88832-971-9 (hardcover)
ISBN 979-8-88832-970-2 (digital)

Christian Faith Publishing
832 Park Avenue
Meadville, PA 16335
www.christianfaithpublishing.com

Printed in the United States of America

Father has a business meeting in Denmark and has taken the family with him. Denmark is a small country in northern Europe. Jeremy and his little sister, April, are so excited!

"Mom, what is that castle over there?" asked April.

"We are going to *Amalienborg Palace.* There we can see a real royal mansion. People travel from all over the world to see it. Danish Royalty are very down to earth and travel around town by train or bus, just like the Danish people. Sometimes when they are here at the palace, they will wave to the crowd.

"Ooh, I hope we see a princess!" April exclaims. "I love princesses!"

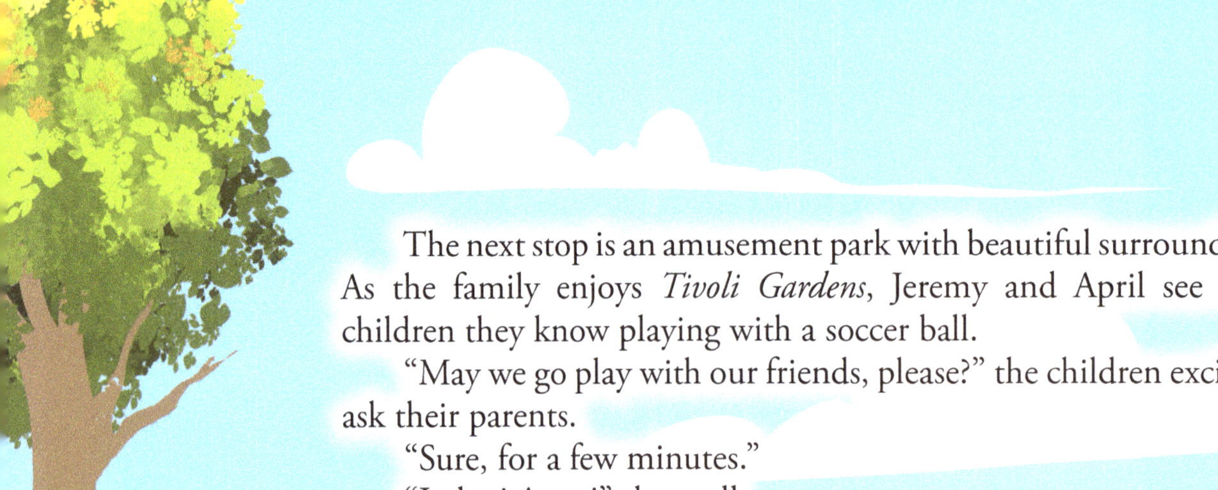

The next stop is an amusement park with beautiful surroundings. As the family enjoys *Tivoli Gardens*, Jeremy and April see some children they know playing with a soccer ball.

"May we go play with our friends, please?" the children excitedly ask their parents.

"Sure, for a few minutes."

"Lukas! Anna!" they yell.

Lukas and Anna spot Jeremy and April. "Hej! How are you?"

"Hello. We are happy to see you. May we play with you?"

"Sure."

They begin to count as they kick the ball back and forth.

"One, two, three, four, five, six, seven, eight, nine, ten."
Lukas says, "We count like this: *en, to, tre, fire, fem, seks, syv, otte, ni, ti.*"
"Danish sounds neat. It's cool how children who live in other parts of the world speak different languages," Jeremy says.
All the other children nod in agreement.
Mother calls for the children.
"It was fun playing with you," says April.
The children say goodbye. "Bye. *Farvel!*"

Later that day, while in a toy store, the children learn some history of Legos. The first Legos were actually made of wood. They were invented by a man named *Ole Kirk Christiansen* in 1932. He made them for his children to play with. The name *Lego* comes from the Danish words *leg god*, which means "plays well."

Legos like the ones we play with today were created in 1958.
"Wow, I didn't know that! It's so interesting learning new facts," says Jeremy as they leave the store.

KAFFE

The family is in Copenhagen, the capital city of Denmark. They are going to see the "Little Mermaid" statue.

The story *Little Mermaid* was written by *Hans Christian Andersen*. Then a ballet was created using the story. It was so popular that *Edvard Eriksen* sculpted a statue out of bronze. The statue of the "Little Mermaid" is only four- feet tall. It sits on a rock, on the shore of the Langelinie cruise harbor.

The statue seen today is actually a copy. The Eriksen family has the original. There are copies of the statue around the world.

Hans Christian Andersen wrote many fairy tales. Some well-known ones are *The Ugly Duckling* and *Thumbelina*. He also wrote *The Snow Queen*, which inspired the movie *Frozen*.

"Denmark is such a great country!" says April. "I want to watch *Frozen* and *The Little Mermaid* when we get home!"

"We did learn a lot of fun and interesting things in Denmark," said Jeremy. "I can't believe that Legos were invented here. I will remember that every time I play with mine."

En
To
Tre
Fire
Fem

Seks

Syv

Otte

Ni

Ti

"We can't wait for our next adventure!" The children began to sing:

I love to learn new things,
I love to go to new places,
I love new adventures,
I love to see happy faces!

A Note to Parents

The author wishes to thank you for selecting this book. The intent is for children to be exposed to the sights and sounds in a country other than their own.

It is suggested that you go online to hear counting in Danish. Listening to a foreign language empowers a young child to expand his worldview. Practice saying *hello* and *goodbye*. Children get excited sharing with others that they have learned new words, especially when they are in another language.

About the Author

Sirpa White was born in Helsinki, Finland. When she was a young child, her family left Finland and moved to the United States. They settled in south Florida. Sirpa grew up and still lives in south Florida.

Sirpa worked as a preschool teacher, and then she became the Director of Admissions for a private Christian school in Lake Worth, of which she was a founding member. During her twenty-five years at the school, she organized many book fairs and fundraisers to purchase books for the children to read. Realizing the importance of children's books, she created their first library.

Always reading to her children, grandchildren, and students, she saw how influential reading was. Reading sparked their imaginations, increased their vocabulary, and exposed them to the big world around them. This love of reading to children grew into a desire to write.

In addition to writing, Sirpa enjoys morning walks, cooking, playing word games, traveling, and spending time with her husband, children, and grandchildren.